Revolution in the Bleachers

More Sports Cartoons by
STEVE MOORE

Collier Books
Macmillan Publishing Company • New York

Collier Macmillan Canada • Toronto

Maxwell Macmillan International
New York • Oxford • Singapore • Sydney

Collier Books
Macmillan Publishing Company
866 Third Avenue, New York, NY 10022

Collier Macmillan Canada, Inc.
1200 Eglinton Avenue East, Suite 200
Don Mills, Ontario M3C 3N1

Library of Congress Cataloging-in-Publication Data
Moore, Steve.
  Revolution in the bleachers: more sports cartoons/Steve Moore.
    p. cm.
  ISBN 0-02-070191-8
  1. Sports—Caricatures and cartoons. 2. American wit and humor,
Pictorial. I. Title.
NC1429.M727A4 1991   90-24156 CIP
741.5'973—dc20

Macmillan books are available at special discounts for bulk purchases for sales promotions, premiums, fund-raising, or educational use. For details, contact:

Special Sales Director
Macmillan Publishing Company
866 Third Avenue
New York, NY 10022

First Collier Books Edition 1991

10 9 8 7 6 5 4 3 2 1

Printed in the United States of America

In Memory of B. Kliban

"Life *is* a game, boy. Life *is* a game that one plays according to the rules . . ."

—Mr. Spencer to Holden Caulfield
in *Catcher in the Rye*

Disaster strikes when, by a quirk of fate or just plain bad timing, two separate "waves" moving in opposite directions collide.

"Yo! ... Wanna play a little two-on-two?"

What they really discuss during those
meetings on the mound.

"Galluzo, you fool! Do you want to lose a hand?!!"

Bruce is careless with a hot bat and
inadvertently ignites a fifth–inning rally.

"Coach! It's your wife again ... are you here?"

Randy latches the deadbolt and foils Ernie's attempt at an easy backdoor layup.

"Hop out. Your ball landed right about here."

"Now, I'll ask you again ... mind if we play through?"

"Careful. Could be a trick ... "

"I hate it when this happens ... he walks a man, gives up a couple of hits and comes completely unraveled."

VIDEO BENCH-CLEARING BRAWL GAME

"Hop on. They were out of carts."

Ballpark organist groupies

"Yo, Kennedy! Get over here. You've been traded."

"Well, guess I did it again, eh guys? Missed a field goal in the final seconds. But, hey, we're a team, right? Right, guys? ... Guys?"

16

17

Wayne and Dewey were later recaptured, but Andy eventually made his way into free agency.

"Whoa, time out, ref! Carl's experiencing sat-
ellite difficulties ... "

"Yo, coach! You want thick or thin crust?"

Cruising for a bruising

In time of need, you're never alone with the amazing new "Bench Alert."

21

Bench-warmer chalk talks

"You idiots!!"

Naismith invents "Basket," the unsuccessful forerunner to the game of basketball.

Superman, as a kid, was always over-throwing first base.

Bill and Marietta inadvertently purchase
tickets in the nose-bleed section.

"...Then he pulled the trigger ...'click.' He pulled it again ... 'click.' And you should have seen the color disappear from his face..."

With a minute and thirty-two seconds left in the game, Herb knocks over his sixth beer and fouls out of the bar.

"Hang on, Bob! What's keeping Markman?! I guess it was a mistake to ask that imbecile to run fetch the rope ... "

"He's been clocked at 100 miles per hour. Yes sirree Bob, 100 big ones ... and talk about wild? Keeriminy ... wild, wild, wild ..."

Field of Dreams — The Sequel

" ... So far we've confirmed that close only counts in horseshoes and hand grenades, dynamite, napalm and plutonium ... how's about we break for lunch, Larry?"

Nolan Ryan, age 90

Funeral for a golfer

With patience, a good eye and no discernable strike zone, Floyd was able to lead the league in walks year after year.

Fall from Eden: the untold story

"Whoa, you're right, John. It says you should
be holding off to the side."

31

"OK, from now on, anything hit in the water is
a ground-rule double ..."

Thursday, 10 a.m., Massachusetts Institute of
Sports Theory. Two scholars come to blows
over opposing viewpoints.

"Oh, a bottle of beer. Isn't that nice ... but I
asked for a *bug* light!"

BALL
WASH

PLUNGE

BOOM!!

BALL
WASH

After conferring with both sides, the judge rules that the defense will be "shirts" and the prosecution "skins."

Life with a seven-foot center

"Ladies and gentlemen, we apologize, but due to a plumbing problem every restroom in the stadium will be closed for the duration of the game ..."

Roger proves that winning is everything.

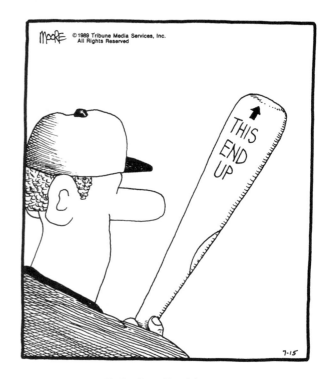

Bats for dim hitters

"Check it out, Helen ... Not only did the quarterback leave the game with stomach pains, now the station is having technical problems ... "

"Sounds like two, possibly three linebackers blitzing ... you'd better toss that sucker."

"... Then it's agreed. As a crowd, we'll be subdued in innings one through seven, then suddenly become a factor in innings eight and nine ..."

MAIN CHUTE
AND
SAFETY CHUTE
FAILED?

NEXT TIME, BUY AN
ACME CHUTE

"YOU CAN COUNT ON IT"

"Coach says to move in a little."

"It's coach. He wants you to relieve Fernwood
... are you warm yet?"

" ... Take a bigger lead. Looking good. Farther, farther. That's it. Not to worry ... "

MOORE

" ... And I believe you'll conclude as I have, gentlemen, that a walk is not, in fact, as good as a hit ... "

MOORE
9-3

44

Proper bleachers attire

The No. 1 cause of head-on jogging collisions

46

Ninja Trout

For 30 years Leonard Figowitz lined the ballfield before every game. For 30 years he poured white chalk in impeccable lines. And one day, something snapped.

Crowd blowers

Hopelessly caught in a rundown, Bill abducts the umpire and demands safe passage to second base.

Introductory Heckling 101

" ... A left-hander? Okee Doke. We'll send him right out ... "

50

"Nice catch, you nitwit! ... Well, I guess that pretty much puts an end to this game for all eternity."

THE IMMACULATE RECEPTION

THE REVOLTING INCOMPLETE

BONK!!

10-29

Every afternoon the moms would gather in the park, where fortunes were sometimes won or lost on a single fight.

52

"He's gaining, Don! Kick! Kick! Faster, Don, faster!!"

"Hello ... Why, yes, I am left-handed ... Well, I'm feeling just fine, thanks ... OK, I'll start loosening up."

Dewey scores a touchdown, but the team is later penalized on the kickoff for the celebration in the end zone.

Safety air bags are introduced to football.

"Point it a little more to the left ..."

" ... And now the socks. We want those
socks ... And no tricks."

Michael Jordan's shoes: The untold story

" ... I'm sorry. You have reached a number that has been disconnected or is no longer in service ..."

Angling in the days before electronic fish locators.

Darryl forgets about his arrangement with Disney.

"Well, Bob, you owe me 50 bucks. He missed the barn by a good 10 yards ... What's that? ... Yeah, yeah. The broad side ... "

PLOOP

A small game hunter in his den.

"Psyche him out, Ernie! Mess with his mind!!"

Golf pants gross-outs

"Now let me understand this ... You washed and rinsed the artificial turf in hot water and then allowed it to tumble dry?"

The intuitive and often uncanny relationship
between a quarterback and his receiver.

Bo Jackson takes up another professional
sport.

" ... And remember, we don't know how they will react to our appearance, so if you see one just stand perfectly motionless ... "

Sir Bob hollows out his lance, packs it with cork and launches a new era in athletic competition.

Stadium P.A. announcers at home

"Toomer! Get your tail out here!!"

Fan Participation Night

"Lola, you'd better get in here. Donald is trying to post up on my Bob again ... "

Because of an old basketball injury, Lyle's knee would often pop out with little or no warning.

Bob enters the wrong data into his computer-
ized exercise bike.

"Keep yelling. Someone's bound to come
along sooner or later."

Roger is embarrassed on the very first day of class in Fencing 101.

"I bagged that one last year."

"You heard me. I'm sick of playing defense. Now just hand me the ball and no one gets hurt."

Caught off guard, the defense was fooled by a fake punt.

In an honor rarely bestowed upon an outsider, the tribe chooses Dr. Colins to throw out the first head and officially open the season.

Arch support groups

"Excuse me, Mr. Oliver, but there are two gentlemen here who would like to play through..."

Words are exchanged, tempers flare and the office rotisserie baseball league once again erupts in a brawl.

The annual harvesting of the fungo bats in Oxnard, Calif.

...WELL, THE PLAYERS ARE COMING ONTO THE FIELD, AND IT LOOKS LIKE WE'RE JUST ABOUT READY FOR THE KICKOFF...

"Do you think you should be messing with
that thing, Larry?"

Running backs in hell.

"Oh, look! Wave to the fans, Lonny. They're saying we're No. 1!"

Bill misjudges a fly ball and falls into the gap
in left-center field.

The first sports reporter

When dweebs get hot

The anguish of choosing sides for debate teams

"Golly, coach. Herbie was just trying to see how much air he could pump into his new basketball shoes."

Introductory Dunk

The infield fly rule

Bob searches for a receiver, secure in the knowledge that his deodorant's invisible shield protects for up to 12 full hours.

Surgical hecklers

SOCIETY
OF
RETIRED
SCREWBALL
PITCHERS

In Dick Butkus' den

After months of training, Carl screws up on
the very first leg of the triathalon.

Early signs of senility in sportscasters

Doug gets up after a knockdown in the third round but is too disoriented to continue.

7-14

"That's it, Helen. Make noise. Rock the boat. Do everything you can to ruin my fishing trip ..."

WHOOP!!
WHOOP!!
KAPOW!!
WHOOP!!

350

SCOREBOARD CONTROL

4-11

" ... Oh, wait! My mistake! Forget the home run. It drifted foul at the last second."

RESERVED   DEVIL-MAY-CARE

11-12

11-7

"I'll be blunt, coach. I'm having a problem with this 'take a lap' thing of yours ..."

Field of Bad Dreams

Steve Moore, who began cartooning at age four-teen in his eighth-grade English textbook, lives in Marina Del Rey, California. When he is not holding down the news editor's desk at the *Los Angeles Times*, Steve gets many of his best ideas for his cartoons while stuck in Southern California freeway traffic. REVOLUTION IN THE BLEACHERS is his follow-up to the highly acclaimed BORN IN THE BLEACHERS. Steve's nationally syndicated strip, "In The Bleachers," is carried by Tribune Media Services in more than 200 newspapers daily.